f o c u s !

by

Chad Earhart

2020 © Chad Earhart
ISBN: 978-1-7361292-3-4

Edited by: Dru Ashwell
Photo Cover: Grace Earhart
Graphic Design and Layout: Sidney McGregor

image: Flaticon.com, pg. 21

f o c u s !

Important Quick Wins to Focus!

WARNING: Thoughts and emotions, even from a book on focus, can distract you. So, I want to give you six principles or values to guide you through this book:

Start where you are, but start. Enough excuses for not being focused. You've got this. *"The journey to a thousand miles begins with one step."* - Lao Tzu

Take small incremental steps. Start learning to focus but take it one bite at a time. I was in a very diverse group of people where one day the leader challenged us to do 100 push-ups. This was a motley crew of old and young, light and let's say plump, etc. We started with one push-up. We then added one push-up a day. After a hundred days, we did a hundred push-ups! Amazing. Find one idea to help you focus. Try it. Learn from it. Try it again and take one more step forward. Come back and do it again. Do that for a hundred days.

Failure is not failure if you learn from it. Did you mess up? Are you not perfect? Welcome to humanity! We learn to walk (or learn to do anything) by falling, reflecting and getting back up and trying again until we get it. Research says you have a limited amount of focus each day, but it also says you can work that focus muscle and make it stronger. If your goal is a million and you only get $500,000 will you be disappointed? If your goal is to be perfectly focused and you only get 50% more focused will you be disappointed? I hope not! If so, it may be time to hire a professional coach or counselor.

If my bullets fit your gun, use them. Not all my ideas will work for you, today, but they might tomorrow. Take my bullets and use them and a month down the road you will be a different person and may find you ready to hear these principles differently. Anytime you are losing focus, pick up this book and choose **one** of these ideas to apply, today. With time, you will find your focus improving.

Coaching questions will help you think deeper and apply. Most people do not like to think. Our education system has failed us in this. I was taught to regurgitate information. My teachers for the most part, and some of them have had a profound effect on my life, tell me what to remember and then I take a test based on what they told me to know. We now want microwave information instead of having to think about things or God forbid changing anything in our life. A question helps you consider things, and the right question can change everything for you such as...

- ◎ Who am I?
- ◎ What do you really want?
- ◎ Why do you want what you want?

You will find these questions labeled

Focus Pocus Coaching Questions

This is a safe place. There are no judgments here. This is a place where you can explore your deeper thoughts and hopes. I work with many people through their "stuff" and everyone has "stuff" by the way. Yes, even the pope.

I find that the best way to help most people is to create safety and give them permission to share what they really think and feel. I work with people with high aspirations, expectations and dreams. I also work with a lot of people who will self-criticize quickly, who have guilt and shame and who have considered being vulnerable, have considered sharing their inner thoughts and dreams and have decided it was not worth it. This is a tragedy.

Not everyone is safe to be vulnerable with and not everyone deserves your trust, but I hope to be a place where you can explore, consider, and be honest with your deeper places of your heart.

Go to chadearhart.com/focuspocus for more insights and freebies.

What is FOCUS POCUS?

It is not unusual for me to say to myself, "Focus Pocus."

I have struggled with focus and awareness as far back as I can remember. I used to be that kid that would periodically drift off and think about things in school oblivious to what was going on around me.

In kindergarten, there was a kid in my class who was whistling.

I thought how cool that was and considered how he did that. I watched how he whistled, puckered my lips, and considered how blowing out could make a sound. Suddenly... "CHAD! Why are you not paying attention?!" My body jolted and a shot of adrenaline coursed through my veins with me thinking, "I was paying attention, attention to this cool kid."

My teacher demanded I go to the principal's office for doing something I didn't even know how to do. That was when I knew this school thing was probably not going to go super well for me. I learned early that I had to figure out a better way to focus or at least let some people think I was focusing.

Fast forward, I learned to be perceived as focusing. I learned to "pay attention" more in school and I tried to hear (not necessarily listen) to what my teachers were saying. I learned to look the teacher in the eyes, smile and nod my head up and down slightly as if to say, "That is so interesting."

I learned that my brain would **focus and engage more when my knee was going up and down 100 miles an hour.** Unfortunately, I often was in trouble for that one thing that helped me focus.

Today, ask my family and they will all say I still have some of these quirks. I still bob my knee up and down, **I bite my finger until I can feel a bit of pain** which is one of my favorite focus pocus strategies, and I say to myself often out loud, "Focus Pocus!" "Focus Pocus!" "Focus POCUS!!" and that repeated phrase helps get my thoughts to "ATTENTION!"

Over time, simple customs and some of the powerful tips in this book have helped me engage my thoughts back into the present and allow me to accomplish what I want in my life in spite of what many call a disability, or as I like to think of them as a *different* ability, called ADHD (adult attention-deficit/hyperactivity disorder) or still by a few ADD.

When understood, ADHD can be a superpower. But like superheroes, we must learn to live in the human world.

I have always had the mindset that all things are possible and so no matter my situation, it can be figured out and I can succeed. All things are possible, but not all things are easy.

My desire for you is that no matter what challenges or frustrations you have when it comes to focusing on what you want for your life, **you will find hope and with time, a process that works for you to accomplish what you want** regardless of your present ability to stay engaged.

Focus Pocus Coaching Questions

At the end of each section, there are **Focus Pocus Coaching Questions** to help you reflect and apply the learning in each chapter.

These questions use the principle of reflective learning.

Research shows that reflective learning is a proven academic practice that helps you focus, apply learning and succeed.

Anyone can "know" something, but that does not mean they apply it. How many times have you read a book just like this one (if you read it at all), but never actually applied much of it?

I already know what a doctor is going to tell me. Be healthy which means exercise more, eat better, and stop doing bad things like smoking. Most of us "know" this, but we are not actually doing it.

My hope is that some of these simple reflective questions will help you apply these tips. It saddens me that most of you will not take the time and effort it takes to use the tools here to help you. Keep using your head to knock down a tree if you wish. Your success will go up proportionally to how much reflection time you add into the back end of your reading.

"Reflection is looking backward so the view looking forward is even clearer." That sounds like focus. Yeah?

Reflecting on the questions at the end of each tip is the hard work that will pay you the most dividends. So, let's practice.

Reflect, answer and write down each of the following questions. Seriously. Do it now!

Focus Pocus Coaching Questions

So far, from what we have discussed, what stands out to you the most?

What kind of growth plan do you have presently? A growth plan

is a process for helping you daily grow into the person that can

focus and accomplish what you want in your life?

1. If you do not know what a growth plan is or don't have a growth plan, go to chadearhart.com/growth to learn what the growth process is and to help you create a structured way of thinking and doing to keep you motivated and focused. Goto chadearhart.com/focuspocus for more insights and freebies.

    ◎ What is the one thing you really want to accomplish in your life or business? Write it down here: (Seriously, write in the book. It's okay.)

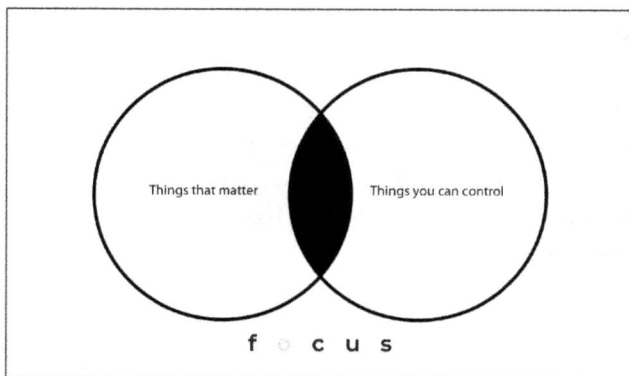

Things that matter   Things you can control

f   c   u   s

FOCUS is

<u>F</u>ollowing <u>O</u>ne <u>C</u>ourse <u>U</u>ntil <u>S</u>uccessful.

Sometimes the "course" you are following requires smaller amounts of time and energy and sometimes the "course" you are following may take years.

Getting your keys before you leave to your car might require a smaller amount of focus energy and time. I do admit that **I have a locator Tile on my keys and on many other important things** so they can be easily found. I have been known to leave my keys and other important things in simple places and it turns into an Easter egg hunt at very inopportune times.

Sometimes your "course" may take years like in accomplishing a project at work or a lifelong dream or goal.

I want to help you find and use your focus muscles so you can finish your course, your goal, your plan, your calling or whatever it is that is important for you to complete.

The apostle Paul in the Bible once said, *"I have fought a good fight, I have finished my **course**..."* Wouldn't that be cool to say that at the end of your life?

I wrote this book during the initial Covid 19 pandemic. Most of the world, today, is inside their home while a virus is looming outside.

It is weird.

Most people are trying to figure out what to do with themselves. The question most are asking is,

Where do I focus my attention?

On survival?

On decompressing?

On family?

On things we have always wanted to do?

We have so many choices at any given moment!

Often, we get overwhelmed or fear kicks in and we don't move at all.

When I first heard the "bad news" of this pandemic, fear kicked in and I got really, really FOCUSED which is my first tip.

ON FEAR & GRATEFULNESS

F.O.C.U.S. Tip # 1 - Use fear only to get you started and gratitude to give you endurance.

"When you are grateful, fear disappears, and abundance appears." - **Tony Robbins**

In this book, I will try not to spend too much time on the research, on long illustrations or too much fluff because you are probably reading this because you need focus not to get lost in the weeds.

I know some of you need more proof than others and some of you need more illustrations so you can apply this easier to your life. So, feel free to contact me about the questions you have, and I will provide a way to help you with clarity, direction or ongoing focus.

- My goal is to get you focused fast. **There are a plethora of resources and research you can look up on your own if and when you want. Fair?**
- My second goal is also to help you focus for the long run so you can accomplish what you really want, your dreams.

Science confirms that fear is an initial motivator. Fear produces hormones and chemicals in our brain and body. These chemicals help sharpen our focus.

For me, during the initial pandemic warning, preservation kicked in initially and helped me get serious enough to act. I realized that the most important thing for me is water. I could not live without water, so I immediately bought a LifeStraw water filtration system. It seems that many people feared not having toilet paper.

Fear can be used initially to get you focused, but it will not help you after that initial adrenaline surge; in fact **fear can be detrimental to your success and is usually what derails people from focus.**

I slowed down my thoughts and quieted the many voices in my head. I then started slowing the negative implications of fear **with gratitude.**

Instead of being run by the latest news fear and being taken off track from the course I had been on, I slowed my thoughts down with gratitude. Gratitude took away the feelings of fear so I could think clearly and make rational next step decisions. When in fear mode, I almost always make poor judgments that derail me from what would be best in the long run.

Worry, for the most part, is a waste of energy because it causes you to clutter your mind with negative energy thinking about things that have not actually happened.

I am not saying ignore warning signs. I am saying **do not let irrational fear run your life.** I was with a friend who lives in deer country in Missouri. She slowed down on the Golden Gate Bridge because she was afraid a deer would jump out in front of her car...on the bridge!

In this book, I am going to give you some great tools to help you focus. If I am honest with you, I know your lack of focus and even more importantly, your lack of accomplishment for your life goes much deeper than needing more tips and tools. Tools can help you, but not if you don't know how to use them.

The reason why I started a coaching company is because I have learned that we primarily run on unconscious thinking or defaults from our past and our childhood. Fears from the hurts of our past kick in as a default and will keep you in a cycle, good or bad, until you can change the default. Professional coaching (with some reflective counseling) is the single best and fastest way I know of to uncover what is going on in your unconscious thinking and to help you make new intentional decisions to get what you want for your life or business as you move forward.

If you have typical shoes and feet, you probably tie your shoes without thinking about it. You walk without thinking about it. You probably drive, for the most part, without thinking about it. However, there was a time you did not know how to tie your shoe, but you learned to do it. With serious intentionality, you could probably learn to tie your shoe differently especially if you had your arm cut off in a car accident.

I was amazed by how many people would say they could not use certain computer technology before the pandemic learning how when they were forced to.

Coaching helps you make the unconscious conscious and learn to do things differently such as why you are not focusing, accomplishing what you want, etc.

We will discuss the benefits of coaching more in F.O.C.U.S Tip # 10.

For now, I will try to help you with one of the biggest problems most people have that keeps them from focusing consistently: The unconscious fear running their life.

Conscious mind:
What I know and am aware and managing

What I am aware of
and trying to figure out

Unconscious mind:
What I am not aware of
and is actually running my
life

The unconscious voices and scripts that often come from fear will be what typically derail your focus. You learned to drive when you were around 16 and your brain then put it in default, so you don't have to keep thinking about it all the time. However, you could have learned to drive incorrectly. I know because I see you driving on the highway around me. You say, "Well, that's the way I drive, and it is none of your business how I drive."

We learn everything the same way. We must intentionally learn how to do it and then our brains put it on default. It is okay when you learn to do things in a way that works, but sometimes we learn things the wrong way. For instance, we may learn to do relationships in a way that does not work for us. Maybe it is the way we think about money and so we are poor because we have a default that says being rich is wrong.

> "Until you make the unconscious, conscious,
> it will direct your life and you will call it fate."
> **Carl Jung** (founder of analytical psychology)

Any excuse will work to keep you unfocused. You might say, "I can't help the way I am," or "This Focus book doesn't fit my personality," "These ideas stifle my creativity," or "There are a dozen books just like this." etc.

For now, let me give you a few tools to help you immediately deal with some of the voices that derail many of us.

Ask yourself the following questions to help you begin to expose some of your unconscious thinking.

1. What do you want? Often what you want is not what you really want. A person may say they want a bunch of money in savings. What they really may want is to feel secure. Maybe a person says they want a nice, new, big, house when what they really want is to be acknowledged by others in the community.

2. What have you learned from your past and what is the truth? Facts are your friends.

Facts from the Past

During the pandemic, I read a few trusted sources of the pandemic of 1918 and a few trusted sources of information on the Coronavirus Disease 2019 (COVID-19).

I am finding these resources to be very accurate predictors as we move forward which allows me to not "freak out" as much on some things and helps me be wise as I move forward on other things.

The Truth about Me and My Past

I am not sure where it began, but I grew up with a belief that I am not enough. I think it stemmed back early when my parents had me very young and the shame around me being born "out of wedlock," a bastard child. Wherever it came from, that feeling of not being enough caused me to overwork and try to please this invisible bar of expectation. Even when I made it to the bar, I would increase the height. I never felt like I was enough.

The first time I said that out loud, I thought I was going to throw up. I felt shame. I knew I was loved and enough as a human, but it sure felt true. I went through a process of seeing and hearing the truth from my creator. Before that moment, I worried that it might be true and so I decided to never talk to God about it and that fear kept me a workaholic.

Pay attention here. What causes fear is usually a negative experience and that experience sticks in our memory to be brought up as a trigger anytime you face similar experiences and it can keep you from moving forward, from making good choices and cause you to lose focus. I turn off most news because I find it triggers things in me. It causes me to derail for hours or days.

How can you learn from the past, your past, to help create an opportunity to grow? For instance, I learned in the 2008 recession that I could lose my shirt and many investment properties because I trusted people too much. My loss was not really because of people or the downturn in the economy. It was because I did not have the awareness to see the situation as an opportunity and to know how to turn it into an opportunity. There were many people just like me who had a different mindset and awareness, and they became extremely wealthy in that exact same circumstance.

Because I learned from last time, I decided to make this crisis into an opportunity. I wrote this book instead of fretting myself into a terrible reality. If you worry about and look at stubbing your toe, it will happen.

1. **How are you at facing your fears?** When I was a chaplain in a hospital there was a saying that people often said, "Hope for the best and prepare for the worst." Ask yourself, "What is the worst thing that could happen?" Often the worry creates more negative energy than if the worst did happen. Facing that fear and considering that reality in your mind can sometimes give your perspective of reality. Often reality is not as bad as worry builds the situation to be.

2. **What is in your control?** There are so many things out of our control that we worry about. We cannot control our circumstances. We cannot control how people will respond to us. Instead of blaming circumstances and people around us that you cannot control, look to the only thing in your control. Yourself.

> "When we are no longer able to change a situation, we are challenged to change ourselves." **Viktor Frankl** (Holocaust survivor, neurologist, psychiatrist)

3. **Are you turning off unnecessary negative energy?** Pick who you listen to carefully. Maybe you need to turn off the negative news and people that trigger your negative thoughts and feelings.

4. How can I use GRATEFULNESS to break through fear?

In the short run, fear can protect you and get you focused and make urgent decisions. In the long game, it goes against you and causes distraction from focus. Fear causes worry, over-analysis, paralyzing tendencies, and overall is not healthy.

To free up your mind from worry and fear, I encourage you to use gratitude as your best friend. Gratitude leads to a peaceful mind that can make wiser more focused decisions. An anxious mind usually triggers knee jerk random decisions and reactions. One of my physician friends says it is as if gratitude slows down time.

Research is telling us that fear and gratitude cannot be in the same place in the brain at the same time. I am grateful to Paul Martinelli and Dr. Harold Bafitus who began showing me the research on this topic.

"The human brain cannot embrace fear and gratitude simultaneously." **Harold Bafitus D.O. (surgeon)**

Choosing to be grateful every morning and every evening will turn off the fear noise in your head so you can make reasonable and wise choices.

Gratefulness allows you to respond instead of react with unstable, and unfocused choices.

If you are <u>not</u> starting to move toward something that is important to you, why? What will the consequences be for you not starting? Who could be affected by you not taking a step forward? **The pain of inaction usually stings longer than the pain of incorrect action.**

I read an article in Today recently about how the elderly have regrets of not taking enough chances on career choices and worrying too much among other things.

I remember reading research when I was younger about how the older regretted similar things.

If you continue to do what you have always done, you will keep getting what you have always gotten.

Don't let fear keep you from moving forward or keep you from the things you will regret one day. Focus doesn't matter if you are not moving. A freight train will not hurt a fly if it isn't moving. A freight train with momentum is unstoppable.

Yes, focused momentum is better. Light focused is called a laser and it can burn through steel.

If the light is not turned on or if the train is not moving, then it has no influence. Make a choice and learn from it.

Choose to move.

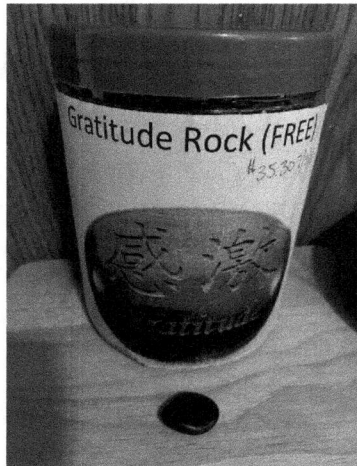

Three years ago, I had one of the most depressing days of my life. It was July 3rd, 2017.

Now, you must realize that the 4th of July is one of my favorite childhood memories. My family used to sell fireworks which raised enough money for us to go on a family vacation which is some of my all-time favorite memories. I love the summer. My birthday is in July. I love the smell of fireworks, watermelon and the smiles and warmth of being together.

But this fourth of July, because of our divorce, my kids were with their mom. I was alone and lonely. I had no job, no money and was extremely worried about how I was going to survive and all around depressed about my life.

It was in that season I was taught about the principle of gratitude and abundance. I made a conscious choice to start being grateful every day instead of letting fear run my emotions and therefore my reactions. I began to see myself as having everything I need instead of never having enough. As soon as I could, I put a hundred-dollar bill on the bedroom ceiling to remind myself that I have more than enough. It did not seem logical in those days to think abundance and gratefulness, but it worked. My attitude began to change. Fear began disappearing and worry stopped having control of my life. I wonder if that is why the Bible verse says, "be thankful in all circumstances." It works. Every time worry is taking over, if I begin to choose to be grateful, fear disappears, and I think better and make better choices. I respond instead of react.

The first F.O.C.U.S. Tip is simple but challenging. Use fear only to get you started and gratitude to quiet your spirit so you can better focus.

Focus Pocus Coaching Questions -

1. How might you use fear to move yourself forward and help you focus?

2. How might you put gratitude daily into your life to help you break through fear barriers?

Go to chadearhart.com/focuspocus for more insights and freebies.

ON EMOTIONS

F.O.C.U.S. Tip # 2 - Know what you really want and make visual emotionally charged reminders.

"You must be the master of your emotions if you wish to live in peace, for he who can control himself, becomes free."
Leon Brown

coach many people through discovering and then accomplishing their dream. A person discovering their why is a key to focusing and pushing through the hard work that is required to accomplish any big goal or dream.

The key to discovering your why starts with knowing what you want.

So,

What do you think you WANT? Write anything down.

I want _____

I have heard that thoughts disentangle themselves through the fingertips. So, write something down. Anything. Just get started. This process will bring your feelings and thoughts to the surface.

Know Your WHY

To get started on a dream or a goal requires only one good thought. Everything you see in a room didn't start in that room; it started with a thought. Someone thought about it and then it became reality with more intentional thought. The paper and ink you are reading from started out as a thought, then someone thought about how to make it a reality.

To accomplish a dream or any big goal requires intentional, intense and often long-distance focus.

Here are some of the top things that help those I coach keep long term focus:

If you want to focus long term, you will need to emotionally connect with the **why** behind your **what.**

Ask most doctor's today and they will say the hard work and schooling are not worth it if you are just wanting to be rich. I have a mentor who says, "There are a million ways to make a million dollars so choose one and focus on it." Being a doctor is not an easy route to take so it usually requires something much deeper to push through the effort to be a physician. It is the same for anything worthwhile in life.

I have another mentor, John Maxwell, who says, "Anything worthwhile is uphill."

Long distance focusing requires you to dig deep and find internal motivators.

1. Remind yourself WHY you do what you do.

> "Those who have a 'why' to live, can bear with almost any 'how'."
> **Victor Frankl**

I call this process the **Five** Whys (Why, Why, Why, Why, Why) Being Wise.

- Start with a big goal you want to achieve for your life.
- Then ask "Why do you want that?"
- After each answer, ask and answer "...and why do you want that?"
- Repeat asking why five times total.

Example - Let us say a 40-year-old lady says...

1. I want a million dollars because I want to buy whatever I want.

2. I want to buy whatever I want because I want security.

3. I want security because I want to focus on helping more people instead of worrying all the time.

4. I want to focus on helping more people instead of worrying all the time because I like helping women especially discover hope.

5. I want to help women especially discover hope because God has helped me find hope and I think it is why I exist.

Usually, in that process, you begin to uncover a deeper level of what you really want in your life and why.

This becomes a deeper motivation for why you want to accomplish most of the big goals in your life.

Then fill in this blank:

My dream is ...

To _____

For me, I want "to live free and help others live free and fulfilled…"

A doctor told me, I want "<u>to be a great physician</u> who gives patient's right knowledge with a compassionate heart and who balances life well."

Janet discovered she wants "to<u> empower women</u> to reach their potential."

One of my kids said, "I want to draw pictures that <u>bring people hope</u>…"

Let that wording of your WHY sink in and see if that still resonates with you after a week or so.

If it does NOT seem to fit who you are, go through the process again or seek feedback from those who know you well or find a good life coach to help you. See F.O.C.U.S. Tip # 10.

If it DOES seem to fit, then find a way to keep that in front of your thoughts when doing what you do.

Make Visual Reminders

- Make visual reminders to help your brain emotionally connect with your dream or goal.
- Making a vision board

Many people have a hard time wanting to do this step but keep reading. Many people experience fear when I first mention this tip because sharing your dream is so close to us personally and sharing it makes us vulnerable... My friend, Dr. John Collins, made his vision board fold-able to protect his innermost thoughts and dreams. NOT EVERYONE IS WORTHY TO HEAR YOUR DREAM. This vision board if mainly for you.

Imagine being on the back end of accomplishing your goal or dream. What is the date? What has happened that shows that you accomplished what you wanted? What pictures, numbers and words would help you emotionally connect with your deeper Why? Where could you put these pictures, so you keep them first in your thinking?

For body physique and health, maybe you find a picture of a guy that has six packs, and you write your ideal weight. It does not need to be fancy, but it needs to connect with you.

Here is a picture a friend of mine used:

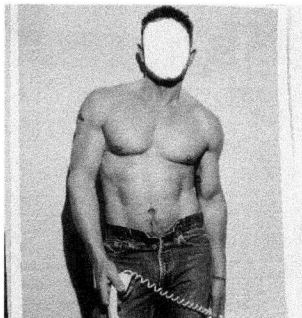

Some people would say, "That picture is unrealistic and that it is not achievable. I will never be able to do that or even 'Do I really want that?'"

This process will help you work through some of your mindset challenges.

Create pictures that connect emotionally with YOU!

This one was made by my assistant, Lorraine Zea.

Your visual reminder does not have to be as fancy as this. Do something.

Below is an example of someone who wanted to describe financial security. The first picture has plenty of disposable money in the checkbook, all the bills are paid and debt free, a portfolio of 11 million dollars, and a safe with emergency cash in it.

See how simple this picture is, but it registers emotionally to this person and he keeps it in a folder close by his side.

Let's say you want to help people find hope. Print off a picture of someone finding hope or mentors who help others find hope or pictures that bring you hope… and tape it on your mirror, above your computer, or add it to the wallpaper on your phone.

I do not want to go into the psychology and research here, but your unconscious mind can be tricked into figuring things out for you instead of working against you. Your brain does not know if your imagination is real or not.

Think of this like a basketball player imagining making baskets day after day even though he is not actually there. Your brain will help you figure out how to make the basket in the real world. I recently started playing Pickleball and started off playing terrible. But in a month, I have improved substantially by hitting the ball on the side of the wall and by imagining where the ball will go on the other side of the net repeatedly. This ability we have is a mind hack you can use to trick your brain into what you want and so your brain will figure it out for you. At its core, your brain is what I call "a figure outer." It simply tries to figure out what it believes, right or wrong, real or imaginary.

◎   Write on your doorposts...

I am a person of faith, but I am not pushing
that on you. I do like to use illustrations when
they are appropriate from the Bible.

One of my physician friends has a Jewish background and one day I saw this piece of metal nailed to her door frame. It was a mezuzah, a decorative object to remind one about a specific prayer to God called the Shema found in the Hebrew Bible. In Deuteronomy 6 and 11, God's people were asked to teach these most important teachings to their children, bind them on their hands...put them on their doorposts, etc. These simple reminders helped keep first things first and top of mind.

By gods grace , I am a

— free forgiven

— desired man of God who is

— enough

butt

and is kicking ~~ass~~ for the kingdom
of God

— wealthy → $10M in 2023
— wise
— diciplined
— Focused

_____

sucessful
effective

That is the principle here. What is most important to you and how can you keep it visibly in front of you every day?

I wrote these words on a mirror that I repeated almost every day in a rundown apartment that I lived. A few months later I was living in one of the nicest houses in my town.

I have put these bands and bracelets on my wrist to remind me of certain values.

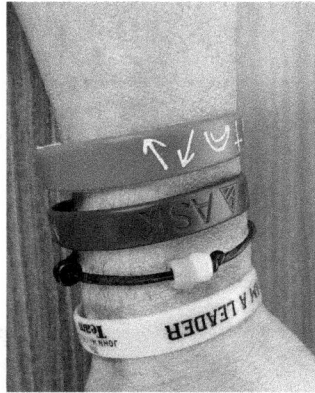

I put these on my bedroom ceiling at one time...

I put that $100 bill on the ceiling when I had no extra money in my bank account to remind me that I have abundance.

The memorials change as I grow.

Don't get bogged down in making your goals perfect but use this as a grid to help you set smarter goals over time.

I think it might be appropriate here to teach you a principle:

Have a bias toward action, not perfection. For instance, if goal setting is new for you, don't get trapped in making perfect goals. Just set a goal and move on it. If you do set goals, use SMARTER* goals or something like it as a template to help you increase how to make more focused goals. Start where you are.

Typically, <u>choose movement over analysis</u>. Choose both but fail forward. Make a choice and learn from it. Don't get stuck in paralysis by analysis.

Trust that your deeper why is guiding you. What is one thing you can do every day to consider your dream, calling, or goal? This focused thought will help your unconscious mind to figure out how to get you there. My mentor suggested I think about my dream and repeat a phrase about my dream 25 times every morning and evening to talk my mind into this reality.

Being on the right path at the right pace will bring you freedom and fulfillment.

The right path is about your purpose, big goals and alignment with your values.

The right pace is learning to go at a speed that is not too fast that you burn out or too slow that you lose momentum.

In the classic book, *Think and Grow Rich*, Napoleon Hill says that *desire* is the starting point of all achievement. Desire is different from unrealistic wishing.

> "Take delight in the Lord, and He will give you the desires of your heart." **Psalm 37:4**

There is a difference between dreaming and fantasy. In *Put Your Dream to the Test*, John Maxwell calls this the Reality Question: Am I depending upon factors within my control to achieve my dream? A dream is based in reality. Wishing causes one to live in a fantasy world and you will acquiesce to playing the lottery instead of thinking into successful behavior.

The wise man, Solomon, said "Those who work their land will have abundant food, but those who chase fantasies will have their fill of poverty" (Prov. 28:19).

I will be honest. I hate the process of setting goals. I also know it helps me focus. It leads me to freedom which is one of my favorite topics and a discussion for another day.

In other words, if you aim at nothing then that is what you will hit and when you aim at something it leads you to more clarity and eventually the adjustments you need to laser in on your ultimate target ...if you do not give up and you are open to mid-course adjustments.

For instance, if you are looking in the general direction down the barrel of a rifle, you will not necessarily hit your target. It is going to get you closer than if you do not aim in that direction at all, but to hit what you really want requires getting your sites lasered in.

You need not only a goal, but some goals in between to reach that ultimate goal. Professional marksman say focus by starting at the site and moving your eyes between the site and the target in the background.

Setting a target AND being open to adjustments will help you be more accurate.

Another way to think about your dream is to imagine being told about the beauty of the Rocky Mountains having never seen them. Going from Missouri to Colorado, you must go through the flat rolling grass of Kansas. At first you can only imagine the mountains. As you come into Colorado, you can begin to see the outline of the mountains. I can imagine the first settlers unsure what they are seeing, but with each day getting closer and it becomes clearer.

I live in the Midwest and I can imagine being in Keystone, Colorado in winter. I can imagine exiting the gondola, seeing the beautiful snow-covered mountain. I can also imagine going

The second year I went to that same mountain, I thought about that fall over and over again. When I started off this time, you know what I did? I fell all the way down the mountain. I had been thinking about that for a year and I did just as I imagined. On that long cold sled ride down, I thought I am going to figure this out. What did I do wrong and how will I adjust my skis and posture, differently? The next time I went down that hill I was very intentional and flew down the hill without falling, exhilarated just as I imagined it.

I am not saying you will get what you imagined every time, but the clearer you can be about what you hope for, the more likely your brain will help you figure out how to get there.

Maybe this will help.

This was the basics of Napoleon Hill's method for turning desire into reality, to becoming rich (and *rich* does not have to be money by the way):

1. Be clear about what you want and make it a specific number.

2. Determine exactly what you intend to give in return for that number.

3. Pick a specific date for when you expect to make the amount in step 1.

4. Create a plan and move toward it even if you don't know how or don't feel like you are ready.

5. Write out clear, concise statements of steps 1 through 4.

6. Read aloud those statements when you wake up and when you go to bed. As you read the statement, experience it by seeing, feeling and believing that you already have accomplished it.

Do you see the balance? Focus on a big, energized goal and then move toward it with persistence making changes along the way as needed.

"If one advances confidently in the direction
of his dreams, and endeavors to live the life
which he has imagined, he will meet with a
success
unexpected in common hours."
Henry David Thoreau

After you know what your deeper purpose is for your life, toward
your dreams, you can then move into what things you want to
accomplish in the future.

Consider this focus trick my friend Matt Bowe calls Unbreakable
Business. He used to work for Apple and helped create LEAN
businesses, but also helps entrepreneurs who are notorious for
having shiny object syndrome.

Pro Tip - Create a Big Picture Power Plan
Board that can always be in plain sight. I was
always forgetting what my big picture was,
who my market was or what goals I was to be
focusing on for the week or day. This tool has
helped me tremendously since I need to have
a visual way to always remember what I am
moving toward.

Here is an example:

1. On one sheet, write down at the top of that page, "3 - 5 Years" representing your envisioned 3 - 5-year goals with a goal end date. On the bottom of the page, write "Vision/WHY."

On that sheet, add three separate sections in the middle of the page with what you think the answers are to these headings:

- Your "Metrics/Goal Numbers" (i.e. 1 million dollars),

- Your reason "WHY" and/or your "Affirmations" (i.e. freedom / fulfillment) and

- Your "Team Partners" you hope to be on your team someday. (i.e. long-term partner / visionary and a full-time integrator)

2. On the second sheet, write down at the top of that page, "1 Year" representing your envisioned 1-year goal with an end date. On the bottom of that page write, "Outcomes/Results/Themes" to describe what you want at the end of the upcoming year.

What are the goals you think it will take to move toward those goals in one year? On that sheet, add the following separate sections in the middle of the page with what the answers are to those headings:

Example:

- ◎ Metrics/Numbers (i.e. 100K in sales)
- ◎ Why/Affirmations (i.e. Margin, to let go of part time job, lower stress)
- ◎ Products & Services (Sale 2000 Widgets at $50 = 100K. Consult 100 people at $1000 = 100K)
- ◎ Teams & Partners (1 Wholesaler, 1 Assistant)

3. On the third sheet, write down at the top of that page, "90 days" representing your envisioned 90-day goal with an end date. On the bottom of that page write,

90 Day   MAY 2020

METRICS

AFFIRMATIONS WHY

TOP 3

TEAMS

- Launch
- Stradegy
- Projects
- Results

"Launch - Strategy - Projects - Results" to describe what you need to do in the next 90 days to accomplish your one-year goals.

What are the big goals you think it will take to move toward your one-year goal?

On that sheet, add the following separate sections in the middle of the page with what the answers are to those headings:

Example:

- ◎ Metrics/Numbers (i.e. 1000 leads, Sales Funnel, Product and Process)
- ◎ Why/Affirmations (i.e. I am committed to **focusing** on this one thing knowing it will lead to the foundation for my future FREEDOM!)
- ◎ Top 3 / Products & Services (Use Ask Method Turbo, Create Signature Product for Doctors, Infrastructure - team, funnel, emails)
- ◎ Teams & Partners (Not What but WHO? VA (virtual assistant, website, Facebook Ads, Copy, accounting, coach, mentor)

4. On the fourth sheet, write down at the top of that sheet "1 Week Action Plan" representing your envisioned next 7 days goals. On the bottom of that page write,

"Backlogs - Biggest Problem" to describe what you need to do in the next 7 days to most likely get you closest to the 90 days goal.

THIS PAGE YOU WILL CHANGE EVERY WEEK!

On that sheet, add the following separate sections with sticky notes under the "1 Week" as headings - *for example:* "Ask Method Turbo," "Create Signature Product for Doctors," "Infrastructure," etc.

Under each heading, add the most likely next steps you need to take to accomplish each heading. (*For example,* under Ask Method Turbo, Do a Deep Dive Lean Survey on 5 people)

This could seem overwhelming to you so here are a few ways to push through.

1. **Get the big goals out of your head and visibly in front of you.** This will help you not have to think so much and be able to remind you where you are when you get frustrated or have mind clutter so you don't waste time thinking over what you have already thought about. Make sense?

2. Working through the process will help you think through details. Just do it or have someone help you do it. This process will be a visual reminder when you get off track. You can always go back to your goal board.

    - Create a visual reminder or phrase to help you focus on every day. What is a visual reminder if you accomplished the goal, the "end experience" that would make it worth it? (Example: Accepting an award, going on vacation, etc.)

    - Write Metrics and specific numbers

My guess is your goals are not big enough. These goals will help trick your subconscious brain into focusing and figuring out how to get to what you really want. Find a specific number to shoot for so your brain will have something to figure out. A goal is not put out there to reach it. A goal is to trick your brain into figuring out how to do what you think you can't. If you aim at a huge number and believe it is possible, you will think differently compared to your goal being to make $7500. What if you aimed at a million and only got $750K. Would you be disappointed?

Make this fun. Get out post-it notes, index cards, construction paper, etc.

I read an article one time about people who have different kinds of workspaces. Those who are stackers or hiders and those who are horizontal or spread out. Some personalities find they lose focus because "out of sight, out of mind" which is why they have everything spread out. These ideas might help those of you with personality types (or with bosses who have personality types) who need a more organized and less cluttered way to keep the most important goals in front of you and therefore help you be more focused.

Focus Pocus Coaching Questions -

1. What is the one next step forward you can choose right now?

2. What are some powerful visuals that you can create and begin viewing TODAY that can propel you forward?

ON THE FUTURE

F.O.C.U.S. Tip # 3 - Everyone has a to-do list. Turbocharge yours earlier.

"By failing to prepare, you are preparing to fail."

Benjamin Franklin

If you aim at nothing. That is what you will hit. Daily, reflect and make a prioritized To-Do List for the NEXT day.

There are lots of interesting stories out there about lists and the origin of to-do lists and their benefits. Google "Benjamin Franklin's lists", "Charles Schwab paying $25K"... to name a few.

I am assuming that you have heard of a to-do list and probably have one of the thousand to-do apps. I would lose focus just searching for a to-do list app and yet this does tell you how popular this concept is in helping people focus.

As Ben Franklin observed, the downside of lists is that they can also overwhelm you.

A good list system is such a simple way to get things out of your head and onto paper, so you do not have to hold them in your brain.

My lists have evolved over time and continue to evolve.

I have combined my list into a multi-functioning tool for reflection. I call it my Daily Do Due.

On one hand, we can get bogged down in over-thinking and not moving forward.

One the other hand, we can get busy doing activities that do not get us to where we want. We can get busy going nowhere.

When I was in college, I read my first life management book. There is no such thing as time management by the way. We can only manage ourselves. We all only have 24 hours. Some people can accomplish more with that time, though. Why is that? There is a reason.

The following diagram helped me become more efficient, not necessarily more effective, but I have still considered it in my life as my tendency is to jump in without thinking.

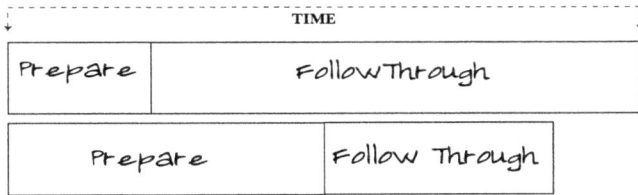

TIME		
Prepare	Follow Through	
Prepare		Follow Through

If I thought about things in advance, it could help me accomplish more in less time. I could go from the post office to the bank to the grocery store in one swift swoop instead of driving all over town. I could make one trip (maybe two) to the hardware store instead of six trips.

I will warn you here that anything to its extreme can be counterproductive.

For instance, preparing by doing too many things at one time or in one day can cause **more** and not less stress and be a loss in productivity and focus.

The principle of **prepare first** can save you time in some situations. The principle of **take action** and learning from it can save you time in others.

How do you know which to do? This is where I recommend Tip# 10 and finding a coach to help you think into what works for you, so you can learn why you do what you do and what is keeping you from accomplishing what you want.

Here is what has been helpful to keep me balanced:

- Daily, I set a time on my calendar to reflect. I remember what I accomplished for the day instead of what I did not accomplish. It keeps me grateful instead of frustrated.

- I then consider the top three things I want to do the NEXT day in order of priority. This process can keep you focused on what is important to you and help you break down the tasks into manageable pieces. This helps you not waste time deciding the next day what you are going to do. It also causes you to prioritize and automatically helps you learn to say no to more things.

- Along the day, I add things to my list of ideas for tomorrow or the things I don't want to forget.

- As you become more aware of yourself, you will learn the things you are good at, choose the things that only you are good at and invest your time primarily on those things. For example, the things I focus on are:
  - ◎ GOD, because I want to honor my Grand Overall Designer above everything else.
  - ◎ COACHING because it is my superpower.

- ◎ CONNECTING because it is how I enjoy and best relate with and sell myself and "service and products."
- ◎ GROWTH because I am a lifelong learner and teacher.

If you prioritize well, the only thing that matters for the day is the ONE NEXT THING. Making daily time to reflect on the next day will eventually help you learn to prioritize better and make clarity for what you want to put on your start doing and stop doing list.

I am a Kansas City Chiefs fan. Sorry Oakland and Bronco fans.

When I lived in Kansas City, one of the coaches, used to say,

"Proper Preparation Prevents Poor Performance." Marty Schottenheimer (former Kansas City Chiefs Coach)

Focus Pocus Coaching Questions -

1. How can you use reflection to help you prioritize?

2. How can you use a daily To Do List to help you with clarity?

ON ACCOUNTABILITY

F.O.C.U.S. Tip # 4 - Find a friend (or friends) to hold you accountable.

"Some friends don't help, but a true friend is closer than your own family." **Proverb 18:24 (CEV)**

For some of you, you may think accountability is a stupid idea. I used to think so, too. If you are a dreamer, it is scary to share your dream for fear someone will shoot it down.

If you are an entrepreneur, you want freedom, and this does not seem free.

If you are an addict, it is terrifying to ask someone to hold you accountable.

I am not saying give away your authority.

I am not saying you will be perfect. You will not be, so the right person to keep you accountable is important.

I am talking about finding a good friend or someone you trust.

I spent decades running from this principle because of why most run from things - fear. More specifically, I feared failure.

I had to turn down voices in my head telling me I am a failure, or I am not enough. How I did this would take more time than one paragraph to explain.

For now, know that you can turn limiting beliefs into liberating truth. Failing is not equal to being a failure.

Are you imperfect? Welcome to humanity. Since the beginning of our existence, we have been falling and getting back up. That is how we learn and grow. When you make a mistake, it is not a failure if you learn from it.

I had to find people who understood this learning process and who believed in me unconditionally. I now find people who support me and who don't shame me; who help me, not leave me.

Now, this requires working through your "stuff" so you can be the person who has a growth mindset instead of an all or nothing mindset. You will hear me say this often, "Tip #10 can help with this."

Once I found the combination of the right inner strength and the right type of relationships, I found this to be one of the most helpful tools for focus.

Inspect what you expect.

I developed a process called *5 Colors of Growth* to help people grow into the person who can accomplish their dream. (available for free at **chadearhart.com/growth**). The Color Yellow represents Light. *Stretch to the light or die in the dark.* There are certain people we need to surround ourselves with to support us and help us grow into the person who can focus and accomplish what we want.

We need guides who shine light on the path ahead, encouragers who come bedise us, and coaches who help us think clearly.

Presently, I now have accountability for almost anything I think is important.

I have a coach who knows my big goals and asks me what I want to be held accountable for, who checks on what progress I made on the decisions I made at the end of our sessions.

I am in several leadership teams / mastermind groups where every week or two we ask each other what our victories are, our top goals we hope to accomplish by our next meeting and where we give each other help where we feel stuck.

I have an accountant and **daily accountability partner**, who happens to be my Dad, who checks in almost every day asking me questions around how my day was spent, billing questions, and what I will do the next day. I also have taught him coaching questions to ask me if I am stuck or overwhelmed from the day.

I have **a best friend**, Dru Ashwell, who regularly checks in for emotional, spiritual and habit support. He is also one of the biggest supporters of my mission in life to live free and help others live free and fulfilled.

I would hope anyone would have a friend like that. Today, I received this quick reminder from Dru,

> "Attention works much like a muscle: use it poorly and it can wither; work it well and it grows."

There is no way I could be where I am today without the intentional relationships that are around me, but it has not always been that way. I cannot begin to share all the names of people who have had a part in helping me on my journey. What relationships do you have, or could you build, that could help you focus and eventually accomplish what is on your heart to achieve?

My relationships did not all start overnight. They each have evolved over time as I have had certain needs and have invested in certain people. These relationships will continue to evolve as I grow.

Focus Pocus Coaching Questions -

1. What is important that needs more focus in your life or business?

2. What one to three questions if asked would help you stay focused?

3. Who in your life could ask those questions of you or who do you need to find or even pay to do that?

ON ENVIRONMENT

F.O.C.U.S. Tip # 5 - Create a sacred workspace.

"Ask yourself what makes you come alive and
go do that, because what
the world needs is people who have come
alive."
Gil Bailie

When the pandemic hit, all kinds of people were working from home. For some people, this was a gift. For others it was hell. Some struggled getting things done and being so close with people day in and day out.

I had learned to work from home way before Covid 19 hit and so it was an easy shift for me, but it was not always that way.

In fact, when I first started, I was terribly distracted being at home. I had three jobs trying to make it and was exhausted. When I was at home, all I wanted to do was watch TV.

I had a very small apartment, my office was in my living/dining room, and I had a window unit for an air conditioner which I had to turn off to hear whenever I contacted people. In the summer, after 10 minutes, I was sweating. I learned to be grateful for the smallest things. I didn't have to commute far to work. It allowed me to get started and it put pressure on me to work hard.

I would later rent a local incubator office for $30 a month that included printer, computer and office supplies. What? Thank you, God! And it was in a basement so it's always cool.

Having a **certain place** with office hours at **certain times** and typical tools like a reliable functioning computer helped provide a place that created emotional connections that would help me focus. These habitual places will trigger new neural pathways (habits) in your brain kind of like muscle memory for athletes.

I noticed that a switch happened when I went to the office. I was there to work. And when I came home, I could then typically switch off. I now have a separate office at my house, that functions the same way. That home office has a very different feel than the rest of my house.

You may have to create a certain atmosphere or environment that works for you.

I realize some of you feel you have no choice in your environment. There are things you don't have control over, but what do you control?

When I was younger, I used to write a weekly talk. I needed a space for focusing, creativity, and where triggers worked for me.

I played with this a lot until I found what worked for me.

I tried changing locations often at first. I was limited by things like cost. I tried my house basement, a noisy and more colorful free local art museum cafeteria and a local library.

Instead of saying, this space doesn't work, can't work, won't work, think what does work and what could work? Experiment and tweak.

Focus Pocus Coaching Questions -

1. What control do you have over your environment? (Can I put on headphones? Put up pictures? Change the location?)

2. How can you use your present resources, colors, music, pictures, routine… to create a designated, "sacred space" for you?

3. What would an ideal space be like for you? What kind of environment distracts you from focus and what helps you focus?

4. What one thing could you do today to either find that space or work towards it?

ON TIME/LIFE MANAGEMENT

F.O.C.U.S. Tip # 6 - Use predetermined time blocks.

"Time is more valuable than money. You can get more money, but you cannot get more time."
Jim Rohn

H ere are a couple of ideas for you.

I am certified through the John Maxwell Team, which at this time in history is the fastest and largest growing leadership development company in the world. One of the tools that they use is what is called the 15 Minute Miracle.

The idea is that you take a week to become consciously aware of where you spend your time and then the next week you build the week you want. You consciously write down what you do every 15 minutes. This will make you very aware. Then, the next week with new awareness, you write down where you want your time to go in 15-minute blocks.

You know how hard it is to do something like that for someone like me?

That process did not work well for me like for others, but it did help me see how fast time disappears and caused me to want to choose how I use my time instead of letting everyone around me or circumstances steal my time.

I realized how much time I give away to other people. Time is something you cannot get back. I was watching a show about Bill Gates. His assistant said he can buy anything he wants, but he cannot buy more time.

I say all of this to encourage you to decide what is important for you and help you move toward prioritizing where to put the big rocks in your life. You probably are familiar with the illustration of two containers and trying to put lots of sizes of rocks, gravel, and water into them.

If you put the smaller rocks in first by the end you will not have room for the big rocks. If you start with the big rocks, you can then put smaller rocks around them, and then eventually you can put in gravel and sand and then water. The idea being that you can get more done if you start with the things that are most important.

So, at first this may seem like it will not work. And like all these tools, don't make it overwhelming for yourself. Choose one big rock idea and put it into your life, your calendar more specifically. Then, consider it. Does it work?

Could you do something different to make it work? Maybe your expectations are too high, and you realize that everything cannot be a big rock.

The idea is not to have perfect focus, but to take one incremental step forward towards focus until you are improving your life, your balance, your outcomes until you are happy about it.

Those of us who are not focused think that calendars and contractions keep us from freedom, but it is the opposite if used correctly. The right structure creates freedom. The right boundaries give us a margin to relax so we don't worry.

Do you have a calendar to help you focus your desired time allocations? **You can accept your life or lead your life.** Be intentional. Prioritize your time.

I use Google Calendar and I block off certain times every day for certain functions. I know that the morning hours between 10 and 12 are good focus hours for me. I work on business and thinking activities during those hours. My phone automatically turns off all distracting reminders at that time. I do not acknowledge emails or look at Facebook.

I now have designated times for everything in my life. Now, hold on for a second before you turn me off. I can change my mind about whatever I put on my calendar, but there is freedom in knowing I have allocated times for the things that are important to me. I designated blocks of time for rest and down time for instance.

Usually there are blocks of time for doing things.

Let me give you an example. For someone out there, you might have this typical schedule.

- 6am - 8am: My time for meditating and getting ready.
- 8am - 12pm: My prime work time.
- 12pm - 2pm: Lunch and exercise (special meetings).
- 2pm - 5pm: Things you do not have to think as much about.
- 5pm-8pm Supper and meetings
- 9pm - Rest and Family

The reality is you need to figure out what blocks of time work for you. What would you like the perfect routine to be for you?

Presently, I have a 10am-12pm time slot that I turn off all reminders on my phone and computer. This is my very guarded time for improving me or my business. Sometimes people ask me if they could have a meeting during those times and I have predetermined this time. I say already have a meeting for that time. The meeting is with me. I do not have to tell everyone who the meeting is for, but I have that choice and I have the choice to replace that time if there is something extremely important.

> **Pro Tip** - In those strategic blocks of time, I sometimes use the Pomodoro Timer. You may have heard of the Tomato timer. You create time spurts, such as 25 minutes and then you take a break for 5.

The goal is to use both awareness of times that work best for you when you have to be more intense and focused for certain functions, putting that in as a big rock of importance, and then using something like a timer to actually improve your focus even more. Using a Pomodoro timer is like focus on steroids.

This is a tool. Maybe it works for you, maybe it does not. There are lots of apps out there that could help you with this.

Often, I find music jolts me into focus. Type in "focus music" and it is usually softer music. That may work for many people, but not for me. The harder the music, the more focused I can be. Maybe it is an ADHD brain or preference. I don't know and don't care. I need to do what works for me - you do what works for you.

What time blocks and tools work for you to help you focus better? Pick one idea and try it for a week.

Focus Pocus Coaching Questions -

1. What are the important things in your daily routine that require more intense focus for you?

2. When would be the best time for you to do those things?

3. How will you block out times in your schedule for those things?

4. How will you respond to interruptions or the people who want you to change your focus and priorities to theirs?

ON POSSIBILITIES

F.O.C.U.S. Tip # 7 - Experiment with ideas before you reject them.

"The possibilities are numerous once we decide to act and not react."
George Bernard Shaw

Sometimes the issue of focus is a competing value. For instance, I had a guy come up to me after a talk I gave after a church service one Sunday. He said he struggled with focus, but said his parents seemed to think that taking medicine meant he was not trusting God.

I took him through a coaching process, and he became aware that he had competing values and needed to figure out what he believed and how they might work for him instead of against him. He concluded that he had two competing values that were something like this. "I value science and free will." "I also value God and respect my parents."

We worked through his beliefs and he discovered a way for him to believe in God, respect his parents and to try medicine that another Christian he respected had tried.

As I mentioned earlier, mindset is usually the bigger issue when it comes to focus. It is not in needing more tools, ideas, or principles. Our beliefs run our actions and if we are not aware of them, they will create confusion or keep us from focus or moving forward.

In Focus Tip 1, we discussed how our actions are tied to emotions and feelings that stem from our unconscious beliefs.

One area that I struggled with for years is the use of medicine. I was stronger than my need for medicine. I should not need it and in an ideal world that is probably true, but last time I checked this world is somewhat broken.

I am also not advocating that you take a pill for everything going wrong in your life. Instead, I want to be realistic here which is surprising...because I am an idealist.

I have a very strong tendency to be distracted, easily. As I typed this, I had four thoughts run through my head including fear of judgments from others, my watch went off and I wanted to jump on Facebook because of a post that popped up.

Besides the typical "Look, Squirrel!" moments that would cause me to forget to even make a doctor's appointment, what often kept me from considering medicine was pride.

If I were really hungry, no amount of distraction would keep me from eating. I may be distracted from eating for a short time, but I will probably eat before the day is done. Yet almost any excuse would keep me from having a discussion with a doctor or psychiatrist about medicine.

After I got over myself and started asking why I would not even consider medicine, I began to do research. I started having conversations with others. I was honest about my struggle with others.

I hate to admit this, but I was over 50 before I even considered that I had ADHD or needed medicine. This has been a terrible mistake and has kept me from the freedom and fulfillment I valued. If I had time, I would share my journey with you from being very unaware and shut down feelings to much more aware and knowing what I feel quickly. It was this healing journey that allowed me to connect with myself enough to want more for my life. My mind was keeping me in denial.

One day, I told my son I would go with him to the doctor because he said he thought he needed extra help to stay focused.

My child was diagnosed with ADHD (attention-deficit/ hyperactivity disorder)

...and I realized I HAD ALL THE SAME SYMPTOMS!

It was about that time, my work had to make major cutbacks. I lost my job and considered it a gift so I could start the dream I had always wanted to pursue. After six months of intense daily "working," I realized I had been working harder than ever, but **getting nowhere.**

I was burning through money, exhausted, feeling like a loser, but determined to figure out how to accomplish and live my dream.

It was in the middle of this incredibly depressing season of my life, I stumbled upon some amazing and very successful people.

This change of perspective and new friends caused me to stop looking at my circumstances and instead consider my choices.

I started thinking, "What is in my control instead of what is out of my control?"

I began testing medicine and the consequences of it. What I have learned is that everyone is different. There are times when I have a difficult time accomplishing anything and other times, I am lasered in.

During a very depressing time in my life, I was on medicine to help me with depression. During certain times, I take medicine to help me focus. Most of the time, I do not take medicine. That could change depending on my awareness and the season. Others need to be on meds daily or not at all.

I can only share with you my story. Maybe you will or will not relate with any of it, but I hope you wake up to YOUR Story.

As I worked through some of my shame issues, I started being honest with a few trusted people. I had a conversation with a physician friend of mine who told me that he had ADHD. He told me the challenges that he had and how medicine helped. He began sharing with me some of the ideas that helped him get through medical school with a distracted mind.

I was so grateful for that honest conversation. You mean a doctor can have struggles with focus, too?

I tried a certain medicine he recommended but did not like some of the side effects. I would go on and off meds frustrated...

Fast forward. I met with a psychiatrist who explained to me why I was experiencing those side effects and how a different kind of medicine would fix that. I tried it. Sure enough, it made a huge difference.

I still have some stubbornness in me and an occasional mindset keeping me from being consistent with meds. I only take medicine now when I find myself highly unfocused. It allowed me to see what was possible and I started creating new habits to give me results.

I have taken natural remedies and try different techniques until I find what works for me.

Most of my family says I ALWAYS need it. So, I must consider those around me. I say all of this to just let you know that there are others out there who struggle with focus and who use techniques including medicine to help them.

For some of you, you have a mental illness or something wrong with the chemicals in your brain. Without medicine, you may not be able to function in society. I grew up with an Aunt and an Uncle who had schizophrenia. If they did not take their medicine, there were major mental consequences.

My uncle once said he was in a band called the Beatles. He was the fifth one and an angel came down and put a radio in his ear so he could sing for the president whenever he wanted to listen. Take your meds. It's a gift.

I throw this tip out for those that I think it might help. It is not for everyone. Be grateful if this tip is not for you. But for the few of you who have shame around something that you did not choose for yourself, your DNA and some aspects of your brain chemistry, I hope you know there is hope.

I also hope you have conversations with others who have similar challenges but have overcome them.

I hope you see that this principle is not just about deciding if you will use medicine. I hope you see that there are options you may shut down before even **considering** them.

I have a mentor who says, "There are a million ways to make a million dollars. Choose one and take a step toward it."

There are a million ways to help you focus...

Focus Pocus Coaching Questions -

1. What focus idea have you heard about that makes you interested but anxious to try? Are your beliefs around those ideas helping or hindering you?

2. How could you find out if an out of the box idea might be a choice to help you focus?

3. If the focus idea does not work, what choices do you have next? Throw out the idea all together and choose something different? Go with the part that works and tweak the idea? Keep doing something that doesn't work for you? Hint - the third option is not a good option.

ON INSPIRATION

F.O.C.U.S. Tip # 8 - Keep inspiration close.

"You can't use up creativity. The more you
use, the more you have."
   Maya Angelou

Inspiration makes me think of nitrous oxide like in the Fast and Furious movies.

There are times I am moving into a stretch of time I want to be more focused or I am in that stretch of time and feel like my focus is slipping. Noooooo! I'm thinking, I have got to push through this!

Before I share this tip, know that there are times your body is saying you need to STOP, and you need to stop. Maybe you need a break, even a quick break. Set the timer for five or ten minutes and then jump back in. Do a quick reward of your favorite snack or YouTube video. Set a timer and jump back in.

Maybe you need a longer break and are nearing burnout. You may need a few days or even more to decompress and allow your body to catch up with your pace. Be aware of your body.

This is needed time I "connect with my spirit." I like to get out in creation and connect with the Creator. A walk, go mountain biking, etc.

I find if I can slow everything down, get away from technology and agendas, dump everything out of my head onto paper, get plenty of replenishment time, ideas begin to surface and then clarity comes.

I went away on a retreat for a week recently and was not allowed to use my phone. What a gift that was.

Okay, I hope you see that I acknowledge the need to slow down at times. More often that not, for me, I need to **push through**. It is during those times I can add **NOX** (nitrous oxide) to the fuel intake of my life to help me turbocharge focus and push through.

I do this by keeping inspiration close by.

What helps "get your head in the game" when you need it?

- What **playlist** can you play (or crank) of your favorite inspirational songs? Do you have some with and without words? What is on your playlist? Send it to me and I will send you mine at chadearhartco@gmail.com.

- Where do you keep a list of **favorite quotes** or new ideas that inspire you?

- Go to and like my Facebook page @ chadearhartcompany for weekly inspirational quotes or send your favorites to me. If I use your quote, I will give you credit or send you a gift.

- What **books** are on your shelf you can look at or read with underlined places that keep you focused?

- What **pictures** can you immediately look at on your wall or on your computer that can help you envision why you are doing what you are doing?

- As a coach, just coaching someone lights my fire. When I help someone struggling in an area that trips my empathy buttons, it stirs something in me.

- What websites inspire you, statistics, people, etc.?

Examples - After my divorce, I moved into a depressing one room apartment, but I started putting up pictures of places I have been or places I wanted to go. I had one simple picture that represented what I wanted. It was of an empty couple's bench in a park looking out at the Eiffel Tower. It signified for me to focus on Adventure, Romance, and Travel.

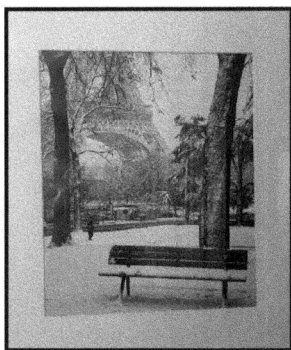

Maybe you use a picture of your family. Here is a picture of mine. It makes me smile every time I look at it.

I put up a picture in my office of a future vacation spot that signified accomplishing my dream.

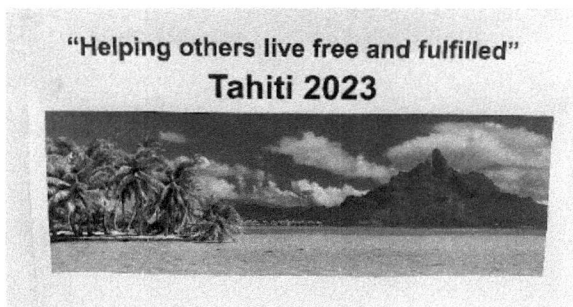

"Helping others live free and fulfilled"
Tahiti 2023

It has long been my belief that amazing leaders have focus and a resilient attitude because they either have an emotional tie in to **a dream** (which is probably connected to their purpose/passion and why) or because they have a **justified discontentedness**, that thing that says "This should not be in the world and someone should do something about it!" That internal drive helps with focus.

Focus Pocus Coaching Questions -

1. What fans your inner fire or gives you energy?

2. What reminds you **why** you are doing what you are doing?

3. Where do you keep inspirational energy boosts like music and quotes so you can get quick access to them as needed?

ON DECLUTTERING

F.O.C.U.S Tip # 9 - Declutter
everything in your head.

"The best way to find out what we really need
is to let go what we don't." **Marie Kondo**

You may have heard of Marie Kondo, the woman who wrote the book *The Life Changing Magic of Tidying Up: The Japanese Art of Decluttering and Organizing.* Her superpower is helping people declutter their living space. She helps a person figure out how to make it a joy to organize all their physical stuff.

I think of myself as the declutterer or the Marie Kondo of the inner world or inner messiness.

One of the things Marie Kondo talks about is having a place for everything. The same is true for your mind when it comes to focusing.

I believe my superpower is coaching. I love inner messiness and helping people declutter. I help people find their inner purpose if they do not know what it is. I help them get clear about their inner world and thoughts and find confidence in next steps.

I like helping people with uncertainty find clarity, those with challenge find solution, those with unbalance find balance, and those with disconnect find what I call REALationships.

One of the common problems with focus is too much clutter in your brain. You are holding too many things at one time.

"Your mind is for having ideas, not holding them." **David Allen**

A common solution is to have a space for holding your thoughts.

Where do you put your lists that are important to you?

Make a list. Tip# 3 is about a specific list called a To Do List. I call it my "Daily Do Due" List. There are many more lists than what you will do for the day. This tip expands on the to do list idea.

Make a list for the many random thoughts that come to your mind. There are lots of apps and ideas out there on how to do this.

Consider what you keep in your head...and typically forget?

Make a list and what would you call that?

- Grocery List
- Christmas Gift ideas for the family
- Birthdays
- Ideas on the book you will write some day
- Movies you want to watch
- Details that need to be done on a work project

Where can you put those thoughts so you can access them later?

David Allen, the Getting Things Done expert, calls these "buckets." Do you have a bucket for the things you would normally keep in your head?

Here are a few places you can keep these lists:

- A real inbox for papers
- A three-ring binder or notebook
- A program that scans and saves items
- Note taking device
- Voice Recorder
- Use a text or email to yourself
- There are endless apps

Personally, I use Evernote, Google Drive and a Three Ring Binder to record most of my thoughts that I want to manage. By the time you see me next, I will have a tweaked system that works even better for me.

What might work for you?

I don't want to go into details someone else has written about, but the point is we need to put these thoughts somewhere so you don't have to carry these thoughts around with you AND we need to prioritize so we can move toward accomplishing something. Right?

If you know what you want and what the next thing is you need to do, then really nothing else matters. All the future ideas and thoughts don't matter until you do the one next thing.

Holding thoughts in your head is a waste of energy.

A key to this is to know ahead of time where you will put your thoughts and to learn to make decisions quickly. So, my encouragement is to create a documented system of how you will do these things. I say documented because it is so easy to forget the process and waste time.

I could write a book on delegating instead of dumping, documented processes and on making decisions.

For now, faster decision making will help declutter your mind so you can have more bandwidth to focus.

One of my mentor's, John Maxwell, is one of the top leadership gurus in the world. He shared how he takes very little time to make decisions -- even big decisions. Usually he decides immediately.

I was at a conference with John a few years ago and he said he was asked by an organization to campaign to be President of the United States of America. The group who asked him was serious and had millions of dollars ready to be applied to his campaign. I think he said he made that huge decision in three days.

I like John's simple process for decision making:

1. What do you feel? What does your heart and intuition tell you?

2. What do you know? What are your options? What is reality? Do you have a backup plan?

3. What do you think? What would be the best choice, today?

John has created a simple process for making decisions.

What is your process for making decisions?

> "Studies have shown that the most successful people make decisions rapidly because they are clear on their values and what they really want for their lives. The same studies show that they are slow to change their decisions, if at all. On the other hand, people who fail usually make decisions slowly and change their minds quickly, always bouncing back and forth. Just decide!"
> **Anthony Robbins**, Awaken the Giant Within, p. 49

Focus Pocus Coaching Questions -

1. What are the "buckets" of thoughts in your head?

2. Where will you keep those thoughts until you are ready to make decisions?

3. What is your process for making decisions?

ON YOUR ASSOCIATIONS

F.O.C.U.S. Tip # 10 - Invest in a professional coach, mentor, and mastermind group.

"Champions aren't made in the ring, they are merely recognized there."
Joe Frazier

Professional coaching is the **single best way** I know of for a person to move forward in accomplishing what they want in their life or business faster.

Did you hear me?

The research continues to show amazing evidence. I see the evidence personally every day.

As I am editing this book, I am watching a Tribute of Anthony Grant who started the Coaching Psychology Unit and Institute for Coaching at the University of Sydney in Australia. I am amazed at how much researched evidence continues to be done exponentially each year on professional coaching.

One of my coaching mentors, Christian Simpson, often shares about how the most highly successful people, the top one percent, typically have these three things to their advantage: a coach, mentors, and a mastermind type group.

You may use a different word but let me explain what I mean.

1. They have a professional coach to help them think into better results. We don't know what we don't know. Coaching helps you discover what you don't know and then helps you accomplish what you want faster. This is a very simplistic definition, but I hope it gets you considering it.

2. They have a mentor who has a proven process that can help them do what they do not know how to do.

3. They have a mastermind group of like-minded individuals who inspire you to think bigger and beyond and support you in your goals, hopes and dreams. This is a simplistic definition as well, but I hope it too gets your attention.

There are many more like minded resources for helping us focus and accomplish things besides these three such as counseling, but these three can have a tremendous effect on helping us focus forward.

I think most people are aware of needing a mentor, but I think many misunderstand masterminds and even more do not understand what a coach is.

A mastermind is about helping those in the group gain more together rather than the facilitator sharing wisdom like in a sermon, lecture, or even in most training environments.

A coach is about helping with goal accomplishment, wellbeing, and focus, but not as most people think. A good coach helps a person get clear about what they want, sets an accomplishment plan and helps them learn from self-reflection until victory happens. This all happens much faster than a person could "figure it out" on their own or even through more education or training.

How many times have you read a book, listened to a mentor or attended a workshop but didn't really apply much of what you learned?

If you go to a doctor for a regular checkup, you know what they are going to say. Exercise more, eat healthy and stop doing bad things to yourself like smoking.

The problem is not that you need more education or medicine or understanding. You already know what you are supposed to do and even what you want to a certain degree, to feel healthy. The problem is that you don't follow through and you can't figure out why.

Good coaching helps with all these things.

Just having this conversation can cause some people to get anxious and create a hunger for potato chips or your favorite "feel good" food. Why is that? There is a reason why we do what we do.

Because of the coaching structure of the alliance between the two individuals, a good coach does not need to know details about the subject's context.

In other words, I do not need to know how to do what you do or why you feel what you feel. When I first learned to coach, my mentor taught us students how to juggle. He asked that we teach our fellow jugglers how to juggle, but with this requirement. We could not give any advice or instruction. We could only ask questions.

One of my favorite stories to share is about Tim Gallwey, recognized father of modern coaching. He was actually a tennis coach.

He recognized that we have an inner world going on separate from our actual actions or outer world. As I learned it, Tim learned skills that he taught his tennis instructors in the early days. He found that they did not work well at first because they always wanted to ask questions in hopes of the tennis players doing what the coach wanted. They would also give instructions like "Keep your eye on the ball" instead of reflection questions that caused the student to think inwardly.

When he brought in coaches who knew nothing about tennis, ski instructors, and taught them how to ask questions in a certain way and with the right attitude, most of the students improved their tennis substantially. And they knew nothing about tennis.

I could share way too much information about the history of coaching, but suffice it to say, a good coach does not need to know your circumstances and context. In fact, I find it harder to coach when I know too much about someone's situation or position.

I learned the nuance of professional coaching from Christian Simpson who taught me that a coach is not a friend though they are friendly, not an educator though they are educated, not a counselor though you will feel like you had therapy and not a mentor though they might put their mentor hat on, periodically.

Let me give you an example.

A student I will call Susie had flunked her first year of medical school. When I met her, she had gone to counseling, had read all kinds of things about how to overcome test anxiety and had an incredible support system and family. She still could not figure out why she could not pass her tests.

We started out discussing what she wanted. She shared about her frustrations. She did not need to share, but I find that most people need to feel heard and acknowledged before they can move forward.

I asked her very key questions to help her reflect on what exactly went on before, during and after the tests. With time, it was discovered that she "triggered" at certain times before she went into the room and immediately after she read a question, she wasn't confident about answering. Her brain reacted and shut down. Game over.

Through questioning, she learned to think differently. She became aware of her tendencies. She became aware of her deeper fears and internal beliefs about herself keeping her stuck. She learned to think differently before she was in that situation again. She was prepared for what her tendency was. She had a new belief about herself and her values. Her next test she flew through. She learned to create new neural pathways.

She went from a 1.9 to a 3.4 GPA and then on to passing her boards without fear.

I have coached a general manager who led the store she managed to receive honors as one of the top 10% of the 1000-plus stores she led.

I coached a single international mom who went from working nights as a CNA and going out only to work, McDonald's and Walmart for six years to getting a job as an accountant and accomplishing her dream.

I coached a guy into finding the love of his life, pastors to growing their churches, CEO's, nonprofits, etc.

You will say, yeah, but what about MY situation? Yes. Coaching can help with that, too.

There are very few contexts where I will not coach a person. I do not coach people through mental illness or serious addictions. I might coach these people, but not these specific situations because they need help beyond my scope of ability. I cannot diagnose a need for and prescribe medicine.

It saddens me to think about this, but most of what you read even in this book, you will not apply to your life. That is why I ask questions on the back end in hopes of getting you to at least improve your likelihood of applying some of the content.

Let me remind you again of one of my favorite quotes:

> "Until you make the unconscious conscious, it will direct your life and you will call it fate."
> **Carl Jung**

That is what a coach helps with.

Some people will ask me how to find a good coach. Here are some questions to get you thinking but do it now before you lose interest of focus.

Some of my mentors: Christian Simpson, Ryan Levesque and John Maxwell

How to find a good coach

Here is a checklist for finding a good coach:

- They have a coach.
- They listen to you and speak less than you.
- They are not primarily a mentor, consultant, friend, counselor, educator and they will not tell you what to do.
- They connect with you on some level.
- They will not judge what you say.
- They can track with you.
- They narrow your thoughts eventually to very practical and focused next steps.

Here are the questions a good coach will probably want to know:

1. What are your top growth goals for your life or organization?

2. What are your biggest challenges keeping you from getting what you want?

3. What do you hope to achieve in your time together with a coach?

Now remember, a mentor is different from a coach. I have had only a few coaches, but hundreds of mentors. Here is how to find a good mentor.

How to find a good mentor.

There are all kinds of mentors. Mentors teach you how to do what you do not know how. A fourth grader can teach a first grader things they do not know.

I have been mentored by some amazing people and they did not even know it. I can be mentored by books and blogs. There are many ways to be mentored.

Let me start by saying much of the following content for this tip is from one of my personal mentors in coaching and entrepreneurship, Christian Simpson.

I have read every one of Christian's emails for years. I listen to what he says, I reflect and work to apply his teaching. He speaks truth into me and ticks me off at times. I am also very grateful for his desire to help me grow. A good mentor will walk you by the hand and help you step by step through a proven process that works.

We are conditioned to regurgitate information. That is not education.

Mentors will help you learn what you do not know step by step.

A coach will help you apply it and help you learn why you are not applying it; help you get focused and figure out the beliefs keeping you from getting there.

Once you find a mentor who you think can teach you, go through this ten-step process.

1. At the end of every week, schedule an hour where you are undisturbed.

2. Think into the gap of where you are and where you want to be. What steps can you think of to do to fill that gap?

3. Identify what questions you need to ask a mentor to help you with those steps or to help you identify further steps. The right question can unlock everything for you. John Maxwell wrote, *Good Leaders Ask Great Questions.* This book can help you start learning to ask better questions.

4. Ask yourself, "Which mentor would best serve me in the question I have?"

5. If I do not already have a mentor relationship, how can I find a mentor relationship with the person who could help me?

6. Are there other ways to get that question answered?

7. During the mentorship call, what can you do to be prepared to make the most of your time together?

8. After your call with a mentor, spend 30 minutes to an hour reflecting. What did I learn from your questioning? What will you do and by when?

9. If you recorded the call, listen to it again and see what you missed the first time.

10. Go back to step one next week.

Successful people are not solopreneurs. All successful people have help from others!

Who could you ask to mentor you and in what area?

> **Pro Tip**: Most of us learn best by teaching others. Who could you teach and mentor what you are learning?

I also mentioned that mastermind groups are helpful.

How to find a good mastermind group.

On your path to success, you will need encouragement, perspective, and feedback.

You will probably pay for a **good** mastermind group, but that does not mean that you can't get started today. Find a group or start a group.

Start somewhere.

1. What is the topic or area you are hoping to grow in? (i.e entrepreneurship, personal development, spiritual growth, real estate development, etc.)

2. Where can you find others who have a common interest? (locally, internet groups, ask your mentor or coach, etc.)

3. Then, ask them if they have a mastermind or start one with them.

4. Read the classic book on Mastermind groups, Think and Grow Rich by Napoleon Hill.

5. To get started, until you understand the concept and find such a group, consider a Triad where you regularly meet with two other people where you:
   - Share your wins.
   - Share your goals for that period.
   - Share where you are stuck.

If you are stuck, have lost momentum, or lack clarity, courage or focus, this tip when consistently applied and with the right people is a surefire way to help you accomplish what you want.

You have probably heard,

> "You are the average of the five people you spend the most time with." **Jim Rohn**

The research is showing that you are the effect of not only your friends but your friend's friends.

So, let's go. Focus! Take one next step!

Do you know what you want?

Are you aware of what beliefs come up when you want that?

Who are the people you can bring in to your world to help you accomplish what you want?

I believe you have limitless potential.

I know you can accomplish what you want.

I do not know if you will do what it takes to accomplish what you want, but I do believe in you. You've got this.

Let me know how I can help you.

Nothing happens by magic. This book did not happen by magic. It required consistent intentionality, Following One Course Until Successful.

Things happen by leadership and the hardest person to lead.... is yourself.

It's not hocus pocus just real tips to focus.

Now, Focus Pocus.

Focus Pocus Coaching Questions -

1. Where will you find a coach, mentor and mastermind to help you on the next step in your journey?

2. What will it take to get the kind of individuals you want?

3. What is the NEXT STEP you can take, today? (Ask this every day!)

THE GRADUATION CHAPTER

"Nothing is impossible with God" **Jesus**

At the end of your life, do you want to live with regret or having made an impact in this world for good?

I used to be a chaplain in a hospital and would go to every serious emergency that involved a death or potential death. I learned quickly that every day is a gift.

Are you grateful for the gift you have been given, today?

What is keeping you from moving forward in your life and business?

What do you want? Have you written it down?

> "A possibility is a hint from God. One must follow it."
> **Soren Kierkegaard**

How big can you dream? What limiting beliefs surface when you do dream?

What would it look like for you to achieve what you really want?

Let me tell you a secret.

Many people, often subconsciously, are afraid to accomplish what they want, and it keeps them stuck.

Moving toward your dream or goals is a bit scary. What if you fail? What if you succeed? That might be scary, too, but would it be worth the investment?

What I want for you is to accomplish what is on your heart.

It may start with completing a goal, but you are made for more.

Following One Course Until Successful will help you in so many ways.

It will build confidence and courage.

This does not mean that you will never make mistakes. Making mistakes is how we learn. It is not a failure if you learn from it.

This does not mean that you will not pivot. There are times you will need to make some mid-course adjustments.

But overall, thinking F.O.C.U.S will lead you to completions, accomplishments, and fulfillment faster.

It will show you that you can finish something bigger than you thought possible.

It will give you hope, bravery, and self-esteem.

It will lead you to the next step on your journey and show you possibilities.

It will open new opportunities you never considered.

So, don't quit!

One of the most read writers of all time wrote, "Let us not become weary in doing good, for at the proper time we will reap a harvest **if we do not give up**."

This was the same ancient apostle I mentioned early in this book that said "I have fought the fight, **I have finished the course,** I have kept the faith" He obviously used strategies of F.O.C.U.S. to his benefit.

Know your goal and take **one** next step forward, today.

Thank you for letting me be part of your journey to accomplishing what is on your heart.

My dream is to help you accomplish yours.

Go to chadearhart.com/focuspocus RIGHT NOW for continued support and freebies.

If I can support you on your journey somehow, contact me at Chad Earhart Company.

Now go…

Follow **O**ne **C**ourse **U**ntil **S**uccessful

I have a daughter who is in Special Olympics and I love their motto and the overall attitude of those athletics. It gives me perspective.

"Let me win, but if I cannot, let me be brave in the attempt."

Chad Earhart

DREAM | FOCUS | LEAD

www.chadearhart.com

ABOUT THE AUTHOR

Chad is the founder of the Chad Earhart Coaching Company. He has spent his entire life helping people connect their hearts and their brains so they can find ultimate freedom and success in life. First as a father of four wonderful and boundless children, then as a pastor and founder of Legacy Christian Church in Lees Summit Missouri, then for 10 years as a Hospital chaplain. But it was never easy. He was diagnosed with ADHD as a young adult as he found it harder and harder to focus. Now, he's a certified member of the John Maxwell Team, the largest and fastest leadership and entrepreneurship certification program. He currently lives in Kirksville, Missouri where he enjoys spending time with his kids (who are now adults) and surrounding himself with nature by camping and hiking mountain biking, and/or playing Pickleball and Wallyball if he must be indoors.

www.ingramcontent.com/pod-product-compliance
Lightning Source LLC
Chambersburg PA
CBHW071605200326
41519CB00021BB/6876